The SS *Eastland* Disaster: The History of the Great Lakes

By Charles River Editors

The SS *Eastland*

About Charles River Editors

Charles River Editors provides superior editing and original writing services across the digital publishing industry, with the expertise to create digital content for publishers across a vast range of subject matter. In addition to providing original digital content for third party publishers, we also republish civilization's greatest literary works, bringing them to new generations of readers via ebooks.

Sign up here to receive updates about free books as we publish them, and visit Our Kindle Author Page to browse today's free promotions and our most recently published Kindle titles.

Introduction

A picture of the *Eastland* on its side in the Chicago River

The SS *Eastland* Disaster (July 24, 1915)

"And then movement caught my eye. I looked across the river. As I watched in disoriented stupefaction a steamer large as an ocean liner slowly turned over on its side as though it were a whale going to take a nap. I didn't believe a huge steamer had done this before my eyes, lashed to a dock, in perfectly calm water, in excellent weather, with no explosion, no fire, nothing. I thought I had gone crazy." – Jack Woodford, writer

The Great Lakes have claimed countless thousands of vessels over the course of history, including swallowing up gigantic freighters like the *Edmund Fitzgerald*, the largest ship of its day to sail the Great Lakes and still the largest to lie below Lake Superior's murky depths. Given the dangerous conditions and precarious history associated with America's largest freshwater lakes, it's somewhat ironic that the deadliest maritime disaster took place in Chicago aboard a ship that capsized while docked to a pier.

When people discuss deadly maritime disasters during the second decade of the 20th century in which more than 800 people were killed, they're often talking about the Titanic or Lusitania, not the Eastland on the Chicago River. However, shockingly enough, on July 24, 1915, a ship full of sightseers out for a day on the Great Lakes capsized while still tied to a dock, sending more than 2,500 passengers into the frigid water. By the time the ship was righted and rescue efforts were completed, nearly 850 people had been killed.

As unbelievable as the incident seemed, the *Eastland* was actually susceptible to just such a problem as a result of its issues with listing, and on top of that, the ship seemed to have all sorts of bad luck in its past, including a collision with another boat and even a mutiny on board. If anything, the safety protocols established after the sinking of the Titanic, most notably the inclusion of enough lifeboats on board for every passenger, made the *Eastland* even more top heavy and contributed to the disaster. Ultimately, several individuals were charged with crimes in connection with the *Eastland* disaster, but none would be found guilty.

The SS Eastland Disaster: The History of the Deadliest Shipwreck on the Great Lakes chronicles the story of the disaster and its aftermath. Along with pictures of important people, places, and events, you will learn about the *Eastland* like never before, in no time at all.

The SS *Eastland* Disaster: The History of the Deadliest Shipwreck on the Great Lakes
About Charles River Editors
Introduction
   Chapter 1: A Foggy Day
   Chapter 2: Shoes and Boots Clomping on the Gangplank
   Chapter 3: A Dreadful Strain
   Chapter 4: The Boat's Tuning Over
   Chapter 5: Soaked Corpses
   Chapter 6: Strong Evidence
   Online Resources
   Bibliography

Chapter 1: A Foggy Day

"The captain expected a foggy day and began to study his charts in his room aboard the Eastland. He wanted to acquaint himself with the course to Michigan City, Indiana, not a usual destination for the Eastland. Pedersen had just passed Erickson, who was hurrying to his breakfast in the mess room. They had a full day in front of them. The busy summer season was half over. It was a Saturday, and the Eastland sat at the dock near the Clark Street Bridge, not their usual one on the Chicago River. They were just about to board twenty-five hundred Western Electric workers who were on holiday. They would leave promptly at 7: 30 that morning, on a two-hour cruise to their picnic grounds, forty miles away in Michigan City. The Eastland needed to leave on time. After Michigan City, it had to get up to St. Joseph to pick up another load of passengers, then return to Chicago, then back to Michigan City to ferry the Western Electric picnickers back to Chicago. ... Erickson sipped his coffee, unaware that the Eastland would not make any of those ports. Within three hours, he would be thrown into an underground jail cell with his watch stopped at 7:33, the exact moment he nearly drowned." - Michael McCarthy, *Ashes Under Water: The SS Eastland and the Shipwreck That Shook America*

July 24, 1915 dawned overcast but warm, making it a good day for a company picnic. Walter Greenbaum, the manager of the Indiana Transportation Company, was no doubt pleased with the deal he had put together for Charles Malmros and Daniel Gee of the Central Committee of the Western Electric Company to transport its employees to and from the site of their company picnic that day. The previous March, he had written to them that "we shall be pleased to handle your party on an excursion from Chicago, Illinois, to Michigan City, Indiana, and return on July 24. 1915. The excursion to be known as the Western Electric Company Employees Hawthorne Works. The roundtrip rate of fare to be one dollar per adult ticket and fifty cents per child's ticket. ... We will furnish you five thousand adult tickets and 200 children's tickets printed in your name; also 5.000 pluggers for advertising. We would likewise supply you with 200 of our regular window cards advertising your excursion. ... Tickets to be good on our regular steamers leaving here at 10 a. m., returning from Michigan City at 4:15 and 6:30 p. m. We, however, agree to establish a special schedule for you on Saturday, July 24. 1915. providing you guarantee payment for at least 2,500 tickets, at the rate of 57 cents per adult ticket to us." The "Hawthorne Works" referred to the Hawthorne Club, a social and educational organization within the company.

Ironically, the initial contract did not mention the *Eastland* by name, saying instead, "This schedule will provide for the steamer *Theodore Roosevelt* leaving Chicago at about 8 a.m. and the steamer *United States* or *Rochester* at about 10 a. m., returning, steamer *Roosevelt* will leave Michigan City at 11 a. m., and the steamer *United States* or *Rochester* at 4:15 p. m., steamer *Roosevelt* at about 6:30 p. m." This is because the *Eastland* did not belong to the Indiana Company but instead to the St. Joseph-Chicago Line.

There were also some caveats that proved to be quite worrying in retrospect, particularly the one that said, "The Indiana Transportation Company reserves the right to cancel this agreement at any time if any new rules or laws be enacted, compelling material alteration of the steamer, increased expense of operating ship or causing reduction in passenger capacity of steamer below that of past year. Also in the event of Senate bill number 136 becoming operative prior to November 4th, 1915, or, at a date which would materially reduce the passenger carrying permit for the steamers heretofore mentioned."

Western Electric employees were not the only sightseers who would come aboard the *Eastland* that day, as the contract allowed that the "Indiana Transportation Company reserves the right to book other small parties…" However, almost everyone on board that fateful day was somehow related to Western Electric, and unfortunately, the vast majority of those boarding the *Eastland* that day had no knowledge of her checkered past. As it turned out, Greenbaum did, and he later admitted, "I had heard of it having listed one time in leaving South Haven several years ago. In leaving South Haven, I heard that the engineer had failed to put the water ballast in. In going into South Haven, they only had 12 feet of water. The Eastland would go into South Haven with the removal of her water ballast, and as they leave South Haven and enter on the lake they would put in the ballast. I understood at that time that the engineer had failed to put the ballast in and that caused her to list, and also the load on the top deck would have a tendency to make her list. … I had understood that after this affair that she went up to Port Huron and that a number of alterations had been made upon the suggestion of Mr. W. J. Wood, the marine architect. … They removed a number of the staterooms so as to reduce the weight that was up in the air." That said, Greenbaum also noted, "The fact that the boat was being operated was evidence to me that she met the Government requirements. The Government would not allow it to go unless it was fit. … I believed it was a safe boat…"

Later, much would be made of the *Eastland*'s ballast (the amount of water weight taken in or expelled to keep the ship balanced), and when asked about this, Greenbaum replied, "I know in a general way how tanks — ballast tanks — are usually installed. Every boat that carries ballast, the captain and engineer should constantly be on guard, if they have a large load of passengers to carry. I don't know what the Eastland carries. The Roosevelt and the United States have what we call ballast or trim tanks. … On account of the depth of the water and on account of the landing at the dock, for the dock is high and the boat is low. They would let the ballast out so as to bring the boat up to make it easier for the passengers to get up."

Adam Weckler, the Harbor Master on duty that day, had always had concerns about the *Eastland*, and he later told those investigating the accident about a conversation he had once had with her Captain, Harry Pedersen: "[A]ll he said to me was — that was something that I could never get into my mind, I have tried to find out ever since I have been appointed harbor master — why the Eastland does not carry water. On account of the way she trimmed, she is always lunging on the side, she is never ready until the moment she ships off, she always gives a lunge according to the side she is tied, but I know the boat so well, I never was much — I know she doesn't carry water, that is why I have been trying to find out why she did not carry water, the only satisfaction that I ever got was they did not need any water. That they do not need any water. That is all the satisfaction I could get, they didn't need water. On the stroke they can fill their compartments in four to six minutes, they can trim her in fifty to thirty seconds. ...I would like to know from my own knowledge why they didn't carry water, I would like to know why, I have asked everybody connected if they knew anything about the boat, 'Why they did not carry water?' ... the answers had been given to me such as they have been anxious to get out, 'they are dragging on the bottom,' some excuses of that kind, still there is always mixed, there is something wrong with the working parts of the water ballast tanks."

Chapter 2: Shoes and Boots Clomping on the Gangplank

A later picture of the site of the disaster

"Passengers were issued tickets good for any of the ships. Those eager to get to the picnic early headed straight for the Eastland. By 6: 30, five thousand people were massing near Water Street, just outside the Eastland's dock. ... Most of the women, in their twenties and thirties, crowded near the dock with long-sleeve embroidered linen dresses. Their hats brimmed with apples, sprays of lilac, shirrings of striped taffeta silk, poppies wound in wreathes, and black velvet bows. Some had brims tilted in grace, others in flirtation. Men, lugging baggage and picnic baskets, wore derbies and straw hats, suits and ties. Boys in blouse suits and rompers held their mothers' hands. The girls wore dresses and bonnets or bows. They would all be funneled through a narrow set of stone steps between the street and the Eastland. With two inspectors using handheld clickers to count the passengers, people began boarding across the Eastland's white gangplank, four feet wide, eight feet long. They embarked quickly, about fifty a minute, polished shoes and boots clomping on the gangplank, which slowly began to dip downward, eventually a full foot." - Michael McCarthy, *Ashes Under Water: The SS Eastland and the Shipwreck That Shook America*

Joseph Lynn, Assistant Harbor Master, arrived at work that morning anticipating a day like any other. He recalled, "Coming from the south, I went down the stairway, working my way through the crowd of passengers that was endeavoring to get aboard the Eastland, and I went as far aft as the gangway, and they were taking passengers in when I arrived, and I found that they had closed the gangway and they were informing such as were waiting to come aboard to go back and go over to the Roosevelt, at her dock. It was understood between our office and Mr. Greenbaum of the Indiana Transportation Company that we would endeavor to facilitate matters by giving them bridges at any time that the other boats were loaded and ready to go through the bridges that ran inside of a bridge hour. I had made all those arrangements the night previous, and her hour was set for about 7:45, and previous to this I had been in the office of the Indiana Transportation Company and conferred with Mr. Greenbaum in relation to the hours of departure of these different boats — about live or six arrangements. The Eastland was to leave the South Haven dock at about 7:45; the Roosevelt at her dock at 8:15, that is east of Clark Street on the south side of the river, and the Petoskey to go from Wells Street, immediately after the leaving of the Eastland, and leave there at about 8:45, which would make about a difference of half an hour in time between the steamboats. And the Racine was to leave the Roosevelt dock at 9:15, and the Rochester from the Roosevelt dock at about 10 o'clock."

However, not long after he arrived, Lynn began to notice that something was not quite right. "I followed along after these passengers that were refused admission on the boat, until they were all off that dock, up over the stairway, on the approach of the Clark Street bridge, and when I was at her mid-ship gangway I looked over the side, and it appeared to me she had considerable of a side list, more so than I had seen her have at any other time that I have been down to the dock at the Rush Street bridge. ... I walked along there to where her spring line was, and met Mr. Weckler, the harbormaster, and I made the remark, 'Ad, she has got quite a list' — we called him Ad — 'Ad, she has got quite a list,' and he says, 'Yes; it is a shame to let that boat go out with that load on her.' And I looked down the bridge at the same time, about, and saw Captain Pedersen there, and I says, 'Good morning, captain,' and he answered me back, and Captain Weckler said, 'Are you taking in your water ballast,' and he nodded and said, 'Yes, I am trimming,' and he left the starboard side of the bridge of the boat and walked out of our sight…"

Despite the captain's assurances, Lynn continued to be concerned. He later testified, "I noticed that the spring line was particularly tight, and I tested it with my foot; and I walked to her waist line. It wasn't in line forward and I noticed that it had a considerable of a side list, and I went forward to the head line, and it didn't seem long, and came back again, and I think that I had walked over the after gangway this third time, and back to the spring line again, and she had gone over four inches to my idea, what I had seen her former mark, for the water had gone down again, and I would say then she was very close — she had very close to an eighteen-inch list, from observation. She was down; her bow was pretty near off the dock, and the stern was in close to the dock to take the passengers down there. I went forward again to where I could look across her stem, and I leaned against the building, and looked up at her so that I would be perfectly firm, and wouldn't be swaying, and I saw her going, and I hollered to Mr. Weckler that 'the boat is going over, get off; if she goes, we are going with her.' and at that Mr. Weckler appeared by the stairway, and I heard' him holler 'Ed !' and I looked up and saw him coming out of the gangway…"

Believing the old adage that the early bird gets the worm, or in this case the best seat on the boat, employees and others began arriving at the dock at around 6:00 that Saturday morning, hoping to be among the first to board one of the three ships set aside to take them on a two hour cruise across to Michigan City. The picnic had sold out and more than 7,000 men, women and children were expected that day. Greenbaum explained, "My original intention was to completely load the Eastland before I loaded the Roosevelt. The afternoon before I called up McCleary [the government inspector] and told them to be sure and have the Government counters down to the dock and check the people ; I asked him to have a couple of men at each boat. I went over to see Lieutenant McMahon of the Police Department and asked him to detail half a dozen officers. He had a couple of officers at each gangway. She started to rain a little after 7 o'clock, and there were quite a number had a preference for the Roosevelt; the officers were holding them."

Daniel Gee arrived at around 7:00 and watched as his fellow employees boarded the ships, and R.J. described the scene on the *Eastland*: "The crowd was very big; it was impossible to get a seat or a chair. I was on the upper deck on the roof. … I should judge about 800 or 900 people. I didn't pay much attention. I looked but there wasn't a seat there, and it started raining and I went down. There were seats around at different places. I don't know; I didn't pay much attention. When I started to go down. I had to wait probably four or five minutes; it is a narrow stairway and the people were going up. I walked down."

C.C. Kelly and his family nearly didn't go, but they would find themselves caught up in the tragedy. He remembered, "When I first got here, I didn't intend to go to the Hawthorne picnic at all. But everybody seemed to look forward to it so much, and there was so much excitement over it, that I finally changed my mind. It took some time to persuade my wife, for she is rather timid about going in boats; but Harry Thyer's wife laughed at the idea of there being any danger, and finally got her consent. We decided to go out early and come back early, so that the children wouldn't get home too late. So by quarter past seven Saturday morning we had our seats on the Eastland. There were eight in our party - Harry Thyer, Mrs. Thyer, their two children, a girl, 8, and a boy, 7; and Mrs. Kelly and myself, with our two youngsters, Jenny, 9, and Charlie, who is five. We all sat on the second deck, as far aft as we could get."

George Goyett and his sons, Lyle (20), Frank (18), and Charlie (16), were also anxious to begin their day of fun. Goyett recalled, "We got down to the dock rather early. I remember looking at a big clock on a warehouse across the river, as I came out on deck, and noticing that it was just ten minutes past seven. Even then, twenty minutes before sailing time, it was hard to get a good place. I didn't bother to go to the upper decks at all, as I had noticed when we got on that they seemed pretty full. Lyle, the oldest of the boys, stayed downstairs, outside on the dock side of the main deck, talking to some friends. Frank, Charlie, and myself went up to the second deck. Frank went outside, just above where Lyle was standing, on the dock side of the boat. Later, when the boat began to capsize, they simply held on to the rail and climbed out on the upturned side of the boat. Charlie and I went forward to the ladies' saloon, up in the bow. Charlie went downstairs again, and I went outside to try and find a seat. The dock side and front of the deck were, I knew, so crowded as to be out of the question, so I went around on the river side. It was almost full here. There were two solid line of occupied chairs, one against the rail and one against the side, down the whole length of the boat; the space between these was filled with people standing and walking around. Seeing that there was no use trying to sit outside, I went back into the saloon. Charlie, who had come upstairs again, was carrying around a little handbag, in which were our bathing suits, towels, and some odds and ends. I told him to take it down to the cloak room and check it, to get it out of the way. 'You boys look me up when we get to Michigan City,' I told him, 'and we'll all have dinner together.' He went below with the bag. I never saw him again."

Of course, at 7:10 a.m., neither Goyett nor anyone else on the *Eastland* had any idea that they would be doing anything other than enjoying a nice summer picnic. He continued, "There was a chair over by the stairway, on the river side, so I went over; it looked like a pretty good spot, so I sat down. Opposite me was Wolcott, foreman of department 4910, with his wife and a friend of hers. They were sitting with their backs to the glass partition that separated the deck and saloon. Just then Miss Kathleen MacIntyre came in, with her mother and little brother. I told Miss MacIntyre to hold my place by the stairs, and went out on the forward deck to get chairs for the rest of her party. When I came back, we all sat down together. There were several other people around that I knew, and we had quite a little group."

As it turned out, Gee wouldn't even be on hand to witness the disaster: "All I observed was just a small listing, then I went to the corner of Washington — corner of South Water Street and Clark, I did not pay very much attention to the boat. I did not know that until I heard the people screaming and the fire department coming; that is the first. I immediately went and looked for my family. …I did not see any people from the Eastland because my family was on the Roosevelt and the people coming from off the Roosevelt. I was very anxious to find out where my people were; I stood there until I seen them; that is all I saw. … I did not see anybody from the Eastland at all, I was there after the accident happened."

Chapter 3: A Dreadful Strain

"On the dance floor, on the promenade deck near the rear of the ship, the young men and women began to laugh and make a joke of the rolling ship. As it would tilt, they would slide on the waxy floor, giggling and shouting, 'All together— hey!' The lines at the stern, near where the passengers boarded, were released and the Eastland's rounded back end began to ease out into the river. It was then that MacDonald, in the tugboat, noticed a dreadful strain on the three forward lines still holding the Eastland by the nose to the dock. From his vantage point, so close to the Eastland's pointed bow, he could see something almost no one else could: The bowlines, the only things that seemed to be preventing the Eastland from rolling over, were stiff, in miserable tension. Just then, Harbormaster Weckler came running along the dock and shouted to the captain of the Kenosha tugboat: 'Don't pull on her at all, cap. Don't pull on her at all. I am not going to give that fellow the bridge until he straightens up.'" - Michael McCarthy, *Ashes Under Water: The SS Eastland and the Shipwreck That Shook America*.

Lawrence Kramer was an office boy who found the *Eastland* already crowded by the time he made his way aboard: "I started for the picnic with another kid, who works in department 2063. When we got on the boat we saw how crowded it was, up on the upper decks, so we only went up one flight of stairs, to the second deck. It was pretty crowded even there, but we finally got a couple of chairs over on the river side of the boat. The part of the deck where we sat had walls, so that we weren't out in the open at all. We were sitting near the head of the stairs, at one end of a sort of alley that ran clear across from one side to the other. On the right side of this alley was the wall of one of the inside cabins; on the other side were the stairs, and then came the wall of another cabin. We noticed that the boat seemed to be tipping over a good deal, but we didn't think much about it until it went clear over. I remember we couldn't keep our feet, and kept slipping back toward the side of the boat."

R. J. Moore, who was aboard that morning, also described the listing of the *Eastland* minutes before it capsized in his testimony: "When I started down the stairs to go onto the boat, there was a long line, five or six abreast, and as I was going along the side of the boat, I saw water coming out of there; I saw it by the ton [out of] six or seven holes in the side of the boat toward the dock. ... I remarked to a gentleman, they were taking out a lot of ballast; he said. 'It isn't ballast, it is exhaust steam.' I thought it was throwing out a lot of steam. It was about 7:10, and the first indication of the boat listing was about eight or nine minutes before it went down, when the refrigerator in the bar was thrown over with all the bottles and made a terrific crash. I was on the second floor and could see the bottles on the floor from that end, and the boat started to list north, and if they were given a signal at that time, I think most of the people could have gotten off the boat. From that time on, the boat kept listing."

In his book about the disaster, Michael McCarthy wrote about what the captain was seeing as things unfolded. "In the Eastland engine room, Erickson noticed that his inclinometer, a little metal arrow that swiveled as the ship tilted, was leaning toward the dockside. Unconcerned, he ordered his men to open up the valves on the river side, the port one, to correct the ship's slight starboard leaning. 'Boys, steady her up a little,' Erickson said. In about three minutes, the Eastland was straightened up, and the gangplank was level for the parade of passengers boarding. All was back to normal. It was nearly seven in the morning, and the passengers herding aboard continuously had reached sixteen hundred. ... The Eastland rolled. As his inclinometer began to tilt from center to the port side, Erickson started up the engines to warm them. It was a slight tilt, and he guessed that the passengers, whom he couldn't see down in his engine room, were congregating on the upper decks on the riverside. To correct for the tilting to port, he ordered his men to open the valves to the starboard side tanks. Perfectly routine."

Adam Weckler, the Harbor Master for Chicago, was in charge of seeing that the steamer safely left port, so he had a tugboat standing by to pull the *Eastland* out. However, he soon realized that something was amiss: "I arrived down at the Clark Street Bridge at 10 minutes after 7 in the morning, and the boat at that time was listed to port, just coming over, about a 5 to 6 degree list. I stood down on the dock and called to Captain Pedersen on the bridge, and I asked him to put in his water ballast and trim her up. He said he was trimming all the time. In the meantime he had given the 'stand-by' order and cast off the stern line. The dock man ran forward to see what line he wanted thrown off. I would not let him throw off the line. I told Captain Pedersen to trim her up. He held up his hand to state that he was trimming as fast as he could. He stepped out to the outside of the bridge. The boat kept turning, and he shouted to the people to get off the best way they could, and the boat, I should say around in 8 or 10 minutes' time, laid right on the side. Of course, the people — passengers — on board were scrambling to get ashore. Those on the hurricane deck jumped overboard. ... Yes; she kind of listed about 7 degrees and came back again, and there is one man threw his coat off and jumped off the boat. I think two or three people jumped off the port side before she went over. When this took place, those people on the hurricane deck commenced to yell. I ran up on the dock and saw men and people climbing upon one another, and mostly all those people were thrown out into the water."

When Weckler was subsequently asked about what he thought went wrong that morning, he responded, "My idea is, sir, that there is something wrong with the pipes or pumps, there is something wrong with the machinery or the handling of them because they could not get them open in time. I do not think they took in water on the starboard tanks at all. I have understood from the assistant harbor master she had a little list to starboard and they trimmed her all over with the port tank; now in that case they had thrown the water from the starboard into the port tank and could not get it back quick enough, that is my idea. ...if you are unloading in the lake into small boats your rails high, you can take water ballast throughout one side and the other also you can load up the gangways and into small boats, you can control in unloading, you can do it in half a minute's time."

As the potential disaster was unfolding, Weckler was desperately trying to help the captain correct the situation before it got any worse. He explained, "He had given no orders at all, because he did not have time to give orders, he was standing on the end of the bridge, talking to me, when I was telling him about the ballast, and he stepped to the outside railing, with his hand in motion and he told them to get back. When she gave a lunge to port he yelled out, 'Get off the boat the best way you can.' That was after the stern line was cast off, this man ran up to cast off the bow line and the breast line…the tug was not pulling on the line, because the line was hanging in the water and the line from the tug, the boat, the bow, to the bow, in my mind, there was just about enough room for the tug to stand between the stem of the Eastland and the bridge. The tug between the stem of the Eastland and the bridge showed the bow line was up from the deck of the tug— there was no chance to pull on the line. To make sure, I gave more line on the tug and the line was hanging."

While there were many warning signs (at least in retrospect), when the disaster occurred, it caught everyone by surprise. In his formal statement, Captain Harry Pedersen claimed, "I was on the bridge and was about ready to pull out when I noticed the boat begin to list. I shouted orders to open the inside doors nearest the dock and give the people a chance to get out. The boat continued to roll and shortly afterwards the hawsers broke and the steamer turned over on its side and was drifting toward the middle of the river. When she went over I jumped and held onto the upper side. It happened in two minutes. The cause is a mystery to me. I have sailed the lakes for twenty-five years and this is the first serious accident I ever had. I do not know how it happened."

Chapter 4: The Boat's Tuning Over

"Then MacDonald saw something that he hadn't seen in all his thirty-one years. Six men on the top deck of the Eastland dashed to the dockside railing. They had decided to make a break for it, and leapt overboard, grabbing a hold of one of the four-inch-thick Manila ropes lashed from the bow of the Eastland to the dock. Hands hooked on it, they began crossing the fat line, called a hawser, hand over hand, monkeylike, suspended above the river. Inside the tilting ship, the mandolin players and violinists struggled to play, and began to dig their heels into the floor to keep from slipping. The Eastland leaned farther. In the engine room, a chute the black gang used to discharge ashes suddenly dipped under water. The river began to gush in. Some of the stokers and oilers hightailed it up steel ladders and fled with sooty faces. On the tugboat, MacDonald was alarmed to see water starting to gush into the partly opened gangways, the square doorways used to load cargo and passengers. Before he could even shout a warning, one of the bowlines, pulling and pulling on a massive stake, lifted the timber piling right out of the dock. Then a second dock line snapped. 'Get off— the boat's turning over,' shouted Mike Javanco, who was rolling his vegetable wagon across the Clark Street Bridge." - Michael McCarthy, *Ashes Under Water: The SS Eastland and the Shipwreck That Shook America.*

Bob Satterfield's illustration depicting the *Eastland* capsizing

Just before 7:30 a.m., with more than 2,500 passengers crowding the ship, matters went from bad to worse when the *Eastland* finally began to actually capsize. Algernon Richey, who saw the accident from the safety of land, noted, "[The captain] stood on the right-hand side of the bridge, with his hand on the rail. As she went over, he grabbed it with his left hand and climbed over, and never even got his feet wet. At the time she started to list, when the captain gave his orders — after she listed at a 45 degree angle; the passengers on the hurricane deck rolled toward that side. …the people that were on the river side — the port side of the boat — as she stood there, gradually listing to that side there, after it got to the top of the freight deck door — then there were cries and screams and she went down like that."

George Haber was fortunate enough to witness the accident from the safety of land. He explained, "I was standing on the dock less than 100 feet away when the boat began to turn over. Some on the men on the boat were loosening some of the ropes. I noticed one heavy cable still fast to the stern, though. Then the boat began turning. It was perhaps ten minutes in turning over on its side. There were about 150 persons I should judge, on the upper decks and from the number that had gone on board, there must have been many more than that below."

L. D. Gadroy, one of the ship's passengers, discussed the exact instant the ship began to capsize: "It was about 7:10 this morning and the boat was lying at the dock near Clark Street Bridge loading with passengers. We were to leave is twenty minutes and the upper deck and cabins were crowded with passengers. There were hundreds of women and children. I estimate there were between two and three thousand on the boat at the time of the accident. I was standing on the tower deck near the gang plank watching the people come aboard. Suddenly I noticed the boast list toward the center of the river. It rolled slightly at first and then seemed to stop. Then it started to roll again. I became alarmed and shouted to the crowd to keep still. Apparently a majority of the passengers were on the side of the boat and this had overweighed it and caused it to list. Suddenly the hawsers which held the boat to the dock snapped and the officers pulled the gang plank in and refused to allow any more on the boat. At this time everybody was panic stricken. Women screamed and men tried to quiet them. I attempted to reach an upper deck but could not because the crowd and the excitement and ran back to the port side, where the gangway had been. The boat then slowly drifted away from the dock, rolling as it slipped in the mid-stream and a moment later it had turned over on its side.

Mrs. Etta O'Donnell believed (probably erroneously) that the gangplank had been holding the ship in place all along. She told a reporter, "The steamer was getting ready to leave and was crowded with excursionists. The officers of the boat pushed the crowd back, which was around the gang plank in order to pull it in. I think this was what caused the boat to list to one side. It never stopped when it started to roll and a few moments later it was out in the middle of the river on its side. I saw dozens of people drowned around me, but was unable to give assistance. By a great effort I was able to climb on the upper side of the boat and managed to hold on until rescued."

Regardless of the cause, within seconds, cries of joy turned into screams of terror as it became clear that people's survival depended almost entirely on where they were at the time the steamer began to turn over. C.C. Kelly, who almost hadn't attended the picnic, described his group's predicament: "Luckily for us, as it afterwards turned out, we were back of the cabin, so we escaped being trapped. When the boat began to list, I didn't think much of it, for I knew that they often rock like that when they are starting up. And then, all of a sudden, she went over. We all went pretty far under the water, of course. I was the first to come up, and found that we were in a regular cage. The stern rail was on the right, the rear wall of the cabin of the left, and the floor and roof of the deck in front and back. There was a lot of loose stuff floating around, and when my wife came to the surface, she came right up under a heavy chair. She got out from under it somehow, and when I saw her I called, 'Where are the children?' 'I don't know,' she said. Just then my little girl came up near me. There was no sign of the boy, though, and I had almost given him up when I saw his hand coming up through the water right by me. Maybe I didn't grab it! All this couldn't have taken half a minute, but it certainly seemed longer."

As everyone on board realized they were in serious trouble, there was mass panic. R.J. Moore recalled, "I tried to get on the south side; there were a little batch of ladies and children, and I took a chance and went with the crowd. I went through the staircase, and just as I struck the floor, the water struck me. I got up in some part of the boat and worked my way through — I suppose about the width of this umbrella and maybe fourteen feet long; it was filled with women and children. They were all saved. I don't know if any of them are here or not. I was pulled out second to last by one of the firemen. I think he belonged to a tugboat. I hung on down in there for thirty-five minutes before I was taken out. When I came out. I wandered away; my clothes were all torn and I was dazed."

According to young Lawrence Kramer, "The soda fountain was near where we were, over beyond the stairs, and that broke loose and fell down on a lot of people that were piled up near me. When I came up out of the water I could see the portholes of the dock side of the boat right over my head. I got over to the wall of the cabin ahead of the stairs, and stood up on that. There were portholes in the side of that cabin too, and you could see the people who were caught inside. They'd come up to the surface of the water, and look at you, and then they'd go down again. Gee, it was awful! When the boat started to go over, the other kid got over to the other side and hung on to one corner of the cabin that was toward the back of the boat. But a man fell down on top of him and knocked him into the water. After he came up he got over to where I was standing out of the water, and climbed up with me. The ceiling of the deck was behind us, and it had cross beams on it. So we crawled up that. I'd boost him, and he'd pull me up to where he was. When we got up to the top, we could just stick our heads out of the porthole, by reaching over. The other kid went through, and then I got hold of the edge of the porthole and swung over. There was a bench under the porthole, and I got one foot on that, and that steadied me. I managed to get half way through the porthole, and then a fireman pulled me through the rest of the way."

A picture of the capsized *Eastland*, with rescue workers attempting to save people while onlookers watch from land

John Morey's life was spared primarily because of where he was at the time the ship tilted. "I was on the upper deck when the boat began to list. I though the boat was rocking at first, then it kept on turning on one side. I caught hold of the rail and held on as the boat went over on its side. A loose chair swung around and struck me on the forehead. Something else hit me, but I don't know what it was, but I managed to keep my feet on the rails until rescued. There were more than 500 on my side of the boat at the time, and many of them must have been drowned."

Obviously, the primary response of the passengers was one of shock and terror. Henry Vantak remembered, "I could not believe the boat was turning over. About a dozen of the 150 persons on the upper decks jumped. The rest were thrown into the river. I did not see my wife or children after the boat turned. They were carried into the river with the crowd. Someone grabbed me around the neck and kept pulling me. It was a woman, but I could not save her."

Few situations in human experience could be more terrifying than being trapped underwater, and tragically, that was the situation that many of passengers on the Eastland found themselves in. Goyett wrote about the chaos around him:

"I had just about sat down when the boat began to list. It went over so far that my chair slid away from the stair rail, against which I was leaning. I didn't pay much attention to this - simply pushed my chair back again. Then the Eastland began to go over in earnest. I caught hold of one of the stair posts and managed to keep from sliding. I looked over to where the people had been sitting on the dock side of the saloon and outer deck. What I saw was exactly what you see when you watch a lot of children rolling down the side of a hill. That entire crowd of men, women and children came slipping and sliding and sprawling down with a mass of lunch boxes, milk bottles, chairs - rubbish of all sort - on top of them. They came down in a floundering, screaming mass, and, as the boat turned completely over on its side, crashed into the stairs, carrying them away. The whole thing came down on me, of course, and I was carried down to the river side of the saloon, which by this time was full of water. I happened to fall against one of the posts between the glass partitions; otherwise I would have gone right down to the river bottom.

"Just as I slid down I managed to retain enough presence of mind of jam a handkerchief in my mouth, to keep from swallowing any water. I lay doubled up there, unable to move, for what seemed years, until the water had risen high enough to float the wreckage off me. I probably owe my life to the fact that a chair was jammed in above me which saved me from being crushed under the weight of the others who had fallen down. I don't remember being frightened - there wasn't time. I know that I was absolutely sure that I was going to be drowned. There didn't seem to be the slightest hope of my being able to get out alive. It sounds like a joke to say that I remembered everything wrong that I had ever done in my past life; that is supposed to be a myth that is always told about drowning people. But that is exactly what happened to me. At last the pressure began to ease up, and I was able to come up to the surface and keep afloat by treading water. The air pressure in the saloon was fearful, and it was some time before I could breathe properly. The boat was lying on its port or left side. Consequently, as I floated facing the dock, I had the glass partition forming the starboard wall of the saloon over my head, the ceiling in back of me, the port side and the river bottom under me, and the saloon deck in front of me."

Desperately searching for a way to survive, Goyett began assessing his situation. He continued, "I worked my way back until I bumped into the saloon ceiling. This consisted mainly of life preserver racks, so I managed to get my feet on one of the cleats, and, holding on to another, was able to keep my head out of water without treading. I looked around the saloon. Several people were floating around, alive. Among them were five of our girls. I called to them, and they managed to get over to where I was. By resting their hands on my shoulders they were all able to keep afloat without much exertion; they kept remarkably cool. In fact, the only person who had lost self-control was a poor woman to my left, who was also clinging to the life-preserver racks. Her child had fallen out of her arms when the boat went over, and was somewhere down under the wreckage. She was frantic, and kept screaming, 'Where's my baby! Where's my baby!' Over toward the stairs I caught sight of Wolcott with his wife. I called out to him, 'Tom, are you hurt?' 'No, I'm all right,' he answered, 'she has a piece of railing to hang on to.'"

A picture of the overturned *Eastland*

Chapter 5: Soaked Corpses

"A slate sky. The tugs tilted under the weight of soaked corpses being lifted quickly from the murky water. Among those at the river, some bystanders had had an impulse to jump into the chilly river and help, then thought the better of it. … Another man, the one who was supposed to supervise the swimming races at the picnic and who was an expert swimmer himself, swam back and forth for more than half an hour rescuing others. Then, exhausted, he drowned. The sinking just an hour old, the Iroquois Memorial Hospital and other area hospitals were overwhelmed with injured survivors, and ambulances were racing from the bridge to outlying hospitals. For blocks, the streets were jammed, with thousands milling shoulder to shoulder, and cars threading through them. … A stream of trucks and horse-drawn wagons made its way through the crowds, bringing lung motors, tubes, and respiratory equipment. The machines were switched on and rumbled and clanked in a ghostly symphony. A doctor from the Red Cross injected the retrieved bodies, some with eyes closed, some with eyes open, with strychnine, a stimulant. At one point, the drug seemed to spark some life in one man, and the respirators were used to try to pump the breath of life back into him." - Michael McCarthy, *Ashes Under Water: The SS Eastland and the Shipwreck That Shook America.*

From almost the moment the *Eastland* capsized, rescue efforts were underway both from land and on the water. Seeing what was happening, Richey tried to help from his vantage point on land. "I stood with the bridge tender of the railroad company at the north end of the Clark Street Bridge from 7 o'clock on until she went over. I saw her start to list. We commented upon it in every way, commented upon it until it got to the top of the middle deck doors. She got to the top of that and commenced to list more, fast, and the crowd on the boat deck, the hurricane deck, started to the south; they ran to the south rail, starboard side. They ran over and it seemed their feet — probably the boat went faster; she went down quick after that. It seemed as if she were overbalanced at the time. ... Those between decks were penned in underneath. ... I ran over to the middle of the bridge and called to the captain. ...he was on the bridge. I ran over and called to him that the boat was listing and that she was going over, after she got to the freight deck doors. ... The bridge tender and I ran down on the pier on the bridge. We threw in everything we could find that was loose; went down on the dock on the south side of the river; the ship chandlers there threw out coil after coil of rope ; we made them fast and threw them into the river, and pulled out three, four and five at a time. I am a good swimmer myself, even with one hand, but I didn't dare go into the water. They would take one — even a good swimmer; those who came up would grab him, three or four of them."

As soon as he understood what was happening, Lynn, the Assistant Harbor Master, sprang into action to try to summon help. "My first impulse was to get back to a telephone, which I did. And I ran up the stairs on the approach of the bridge, south to the iron bridge, and goes back to the City of South Haven dock, and, arriving on the first floor, I had to go west 150 feet, then back to get up another flight of stairs, and then came in here and got into the South Haven steamboat line's office, and I got a telephone and immediately telephoned the City Hall and had them send all the ambulances and pulmotors and lung motors, and to notify the police department and the fire department that the Eastland was turning over, and that is about an interval of nine or ten minutes from the time I landed on that dock, and I set the telephone down and looked out, and saw that the tug was in close under her bow, and that they were jumping onto that, and the people were climbing over her side — the starboard side — in over the side, and some were jumping out into the river, and throwing life preservers and other things, and the dock men were throwing everything..."

At this point, Lynn made a quick decision that might not have saved many lives but at least represented an attempt to do something that could have made a big difference. "I grabbed a telephone book, hunting for the city boat company, to come and cut holes in her — upon her — between what you would call her second, you would call that the second main deck — that is, her cabin deck. An opportunity to get out would have to be through those portholes — those on the starboard side were going over the rail to get on her side and stand on them, and I tried to look at it, and I didn't know where to look for it, for those ox-welders, because they had to cut places for them in order to get down into the cabin, and I tried the big phone — the regular day company's phone, thinking that they had one over there, and I asked where to get them, and I couldn't get that office, and I came back down onto the dock to assist in throwing all the lines that I possibly could, brought from the docks. The yardmaster — probably he was there, and every description of things over to the boat, and endeavoring to get those people quieted, and to throw the lines around the river side of this to those who were in the water, and went over to La Salle street, then to South Water, down South Water to Wells and across the Wells Street bridge down the dock to the Dunham Towing Company, to inquire if they had such a thing there, and I was unable to get this tug company on the phone."

With more than 2,000 people suddenly plunged into the cold water, pandemonium ensued, and policeman Henry II. Scalier was one of the first men to come to their rescue. "I saw scores of men and women, many of them holding children, plunge into the water. I jumped into a row boat and I pulled out to the drowning. I think I got about fifty ashore. The fire boat and tugs hurried to the scene and picked up more than a hundred people. We grabbed those nearest us first. At one time I had four women in the boat with me. Others I aided by dragging them from the water onto the decks."

Gadroy was one of the fortunate ones. He recalled, I climbed over on the side of the boat and stayed there until I was taken out by life savers. Many of the passengers leaded into the water as the boat went over. Scores of others were caught in the cabins and drowned. When the small boats began coming out to us, I worked with other survivors in taking passengers out of the water and cutting holes in the cabins to remove bodies."

Joe Brozak survived thanks to an incredibly lucky accident: "I was with a party of four and they were all drowned. My coat caught on a nail and when the boat went over I was held above the water." Meanwhile, C. C. Kelly and his family were eventually rescued: "We managed to hold on to an angle iron, and I shouted for help. Before long, they let down ropes and got us out. Mrs. Thyer and her boy were saved; but Harry and the little girl were lost. The girl was sitting holding my daughter by the hand as the boat went over, and I can't imagine how they were separated. When I got out and looked at my watch, I found it had stopped. I haven't wound it since. It's just as it was then, with the hands pointing to seven thirty-one."

Goyett lost his youngest son in the wreck, but he and his two older sons survived, and he told the story of his rescue. "Just then the first of the rescuers found us. Someone stuck an oar through the porthole over our heads nearby. The woman who had lost her baby made a grab for it, missed it, and went down. I managed to grab her and get her back beside me, and tried to quiet her. The only way the rescuers could get at us was by smashing the glass partition over our heads. Of course, all the jagged pieces of glass showered down of top of us, and several of us were cut - I had one of my thumbs gashed; but it was the only thing to do. They let a rope down with a loop on the end of it, and we threw it over the shoulders of the woman who had gone under before. She was the first one to be pulled out. When all the women were out I must have caved in all at once. I remember hearing someone call down, 'Come out yourself, George.' I remember, too, trying to put the rope under my shoulders. I must have succeeded, for the next thing I remember is lying out on the side of the boat with an ambulance surgeon down beside me. I tried to get up, but found that my right leg wouldn't hold me. 'How do you feel?' the surgeon asked me. 'Pretty good,' I said, 'but I can't walk.' The surgeon looked me over and said I had a dislocated knee. So a big policeman held on to my upper leg while the surgeon pulled on the lower and snapped the joint into place. It certainly felt fine after it got back! I felt perfectly well, and said I thought I'd go back and help get some of the other people out. 'Not much you won't,' said the surgeon. And before I knew it they had me in an ambulance, on the way to the Iroquois Hospital."

As the luckiest survivors were able to get clear of the ship and others were rescued by the nearby tugboat *Kenosha*, others continued to help on land. Among those on hand to try to help was a nurse named Repa, who later explained how she arrived on the scene: "I was on a trolley car, at Lake Street, when I heard what I thought must be screams; I could hear them even above the noise of the car and the noises on the street. Just then a mounted policeman galloped up and stopped all the traffic, shouting: 'Excursion boat upset - look out for the ambulance!' I knew at once that it must be one of our boats, and ran to the front of the car, to get off. The motorman tried to stop me, but I slipped past him and jumped off just as one of the ambulances came up. It had to slow up on account of the congestion, and I managed to jump on the back step. I had my uniform on, and so was allowed to stay on until we got to the dock. I don't know how I got on the dock, or on the Eastland. Indeed, there are a good many things that happened that day that I am still hazy about. All I remember is climbing up the slippery side of the boat, losing my footing, and being shoved up by somebody from behind. I finally got to where I could stand up on the side of the boat, which was lying out of water."

A picture of the Kenosha rescuing passengers

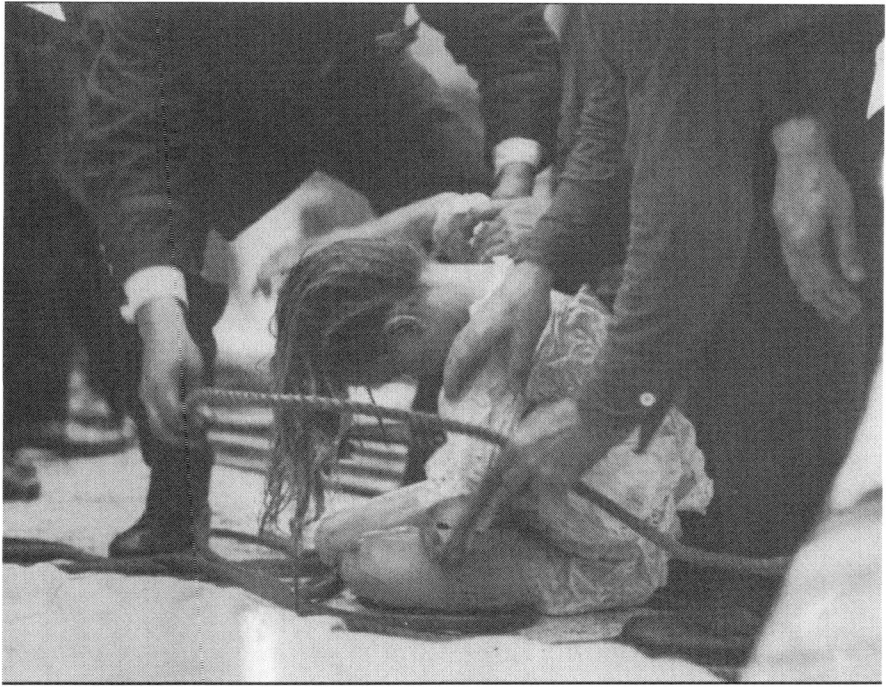

Pictures of the frantic rescue efforts

Even for someone with a strong medical background, the scene at the dock was shocking. Repa wrote, "I shall never be able to forget what I saw. People were struggling in the water, clustered so thickly that they literally covered the surface of the river. A few were swimming; the rest were floundering about, some clinging to a life raft that had floated free, others clutching at anything they could reach - at bits of wood, at each other, grabbing each other, pulling each other down, and screaming! The screaming was the most horrible of all. They were already pulling them out from below when I got there, out of the water and out through the portholes. People were being dragged out, wet, bleeding, and hysterical, by the scores. Most of those from the decks and the inside of the boat were cut more or less severely, because the chairs and benches had slid down on top of them when the boat went over. Those who had no injuries beyond the wetting and the shock were sent to the various hotels."

In spite of her frightening surroundings, Repa put her training right to work. "I started working, first on the boat itself and then on the dock, helping to try and resuscitate those who were unconscious. The pulmotors had not yet arrived, and we had to try what "first aid" measures we could. The injured were taken over to the Iroquois Memorial Hospital. Remembering that this is only an emergency hospital, and is not equipped to handle a large number of cases at once, I asked a policeman how many nurses were on duty there. He said that there were only two. Knowing that I would be more needed there than at the dock, for the present, I hurried over. I went back and forth between the hospital and the dock several times during the day, and had no trouble in making the journey quickly. I simply jumped on a patrol wagon or an ambulance, and being, as I have said, in uniform, was able to make the trip without being questioned."

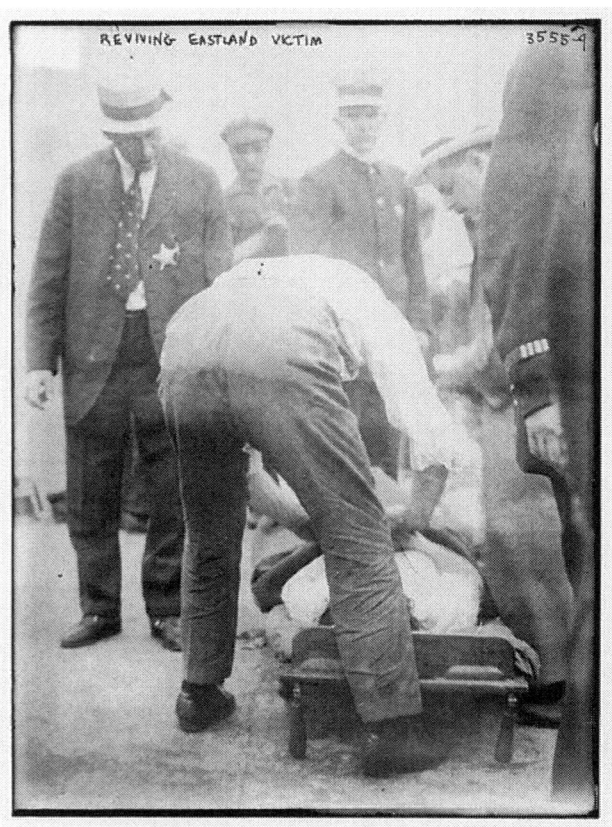

A picture of attempts to revive a victim

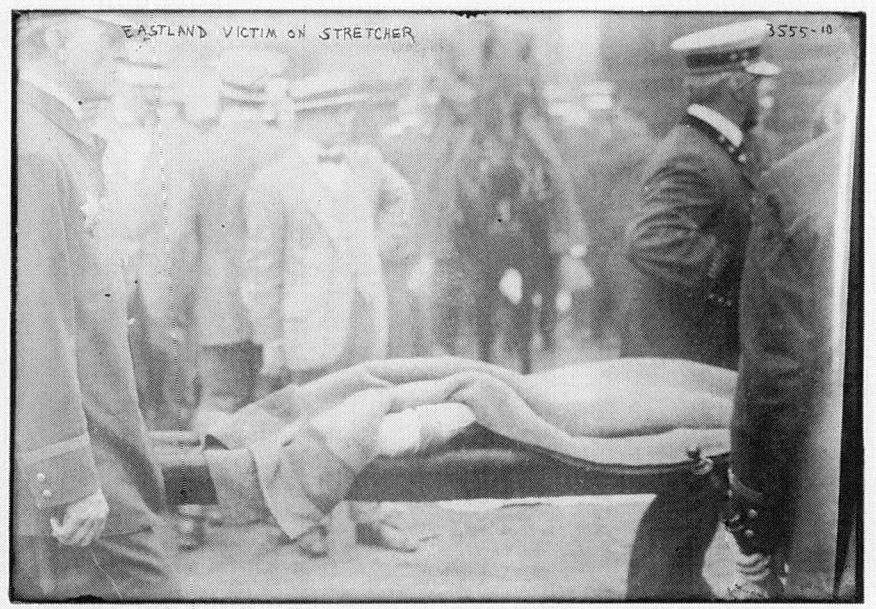

A picture of a victim on a stretcher

Unfortunately, the chaos of her surroundings often kept Repa from doing all that she wanted to. She later explained, "The one place I did have trouble, and a great deal of it, was at the dock. The police had evidently received orders to keep everybody back, and so zealously did they perform their work that I was held up several times until I could be identified. I finally remembered the arm bands that we nurses had received to wear at the picnic. These were of red, white and blue cloth, with a red cross on them. After I had put mine on I had no further trouble."

Things back at the hospital were nearly as desperate as conditions at the dock, but those in the area also rose to the challenge of helping others. Repa continued, "When I got to the Iroquois I found the two nurses distracted. More and more people were arriving every minute, wet and shivering, and there were no blankets left. Something had to be done quickly, so I had one of the nurses telephone to Marshall Field & Company for 500 blankets, with orders to charge them to the Western Electric Company. In the meantime I telephoned to some of the nearby restaurants and had them send over hot soup and coffee to the hospital. By this time the hospital was so full of people that we had no place to put the less seriously injured while they were drying off. Luckily, just at this time, word came from men working in the boiler room of a large building nearby that they would care for as many people as we cared to send over. I must say that the people of Chicago showed a wonderful spirit. Everyone did all he could to help. As soon as my patients were sufficiently recovered, I would send them home, thinking it better to have them with their families as soon as possible. In order to do this, I would simply go out into the street, stop the first automobile that came along, load it up with people, and tell the owner or driver where to take them. And not one driver said "no," or seemed anything but anxious to help out! When the women would be brought off the boat dripping wet, the men standing by simply took off their coats and put them around them."

As the search for the living gave way to a search for the dead, reporters were already quick to the scene. Even as the disaster was ongoing, Mrs. William Peterson told one of them, "I was pulled clear under water and when I came to the surface, I saw two hands reaching out of a porthole. They pulled me through. I don't know whether my husband, daughter and sister-in-law were saved or not."

Just when it seemed circumstances could not get any worse, the weather turned foul and further hampered what had now become more of a recovery operation than rescue efforts. Nurse Repa recalled, "About nine or half-past I started back to the dock. When I got to Clark Street the crowd was so dense that I simply couldn't walk a step further. So I got on a hook and ladder truck that was going down. When I got to the dock they had begun to bring the bodies up from the hold, and it was pouring rain. The bodies came out faster than we could handle them. By this time a number of outside nurses and doctors were at work on the victims. Most of them were dead, but a few still showed signs of life. I saw that if any of these were to be saved we must get them away from the dock. The crowding and confusion were terrible. The bodies were laid out on the dock, on the bridges, some on the Roosevelt, others on the sidewalk. A crowd of willing but ignorant volunteers kept getting in the way, and made our attempts at resuscitation almost useless. I asked one of the policemen: 'Isn't there some building where we can take these people? Some of them have a fighting chance if we can get them in out of the rain and away from this crowd.' He promised to see what could be done, and went away. A little later he returned, saying that we could take the bodies over to Reid & Murdoch's warehouse. We took the bodies we had, and all the others that came out, over there; but it was too late. Out of hundreds that we took to the warehouse, only four were revived."

As the day wore on, the chaos and desperation in the area only increased, and more and more family members rushed around searching for missing loved ones. Repa wrote, "By this time I had on my arm band, and so was able to go from the dock to the warehouse and back without being stopped. What made the confusion at the dock still worse was the fact that many of the people who had been pulled out of the water uninjured were still so dazed that they were wandering up and down without knowing where they were or what they were doing. I found one man up a little alley nearby. He was wandering up and down, with a ghastly, expressionless face, repeating over and over again, "I lost them all, I lost them all." His wife and three children were somewhere in the hold of the Eastland. About twelve o'clock they reached the bodies in the inner cabins; and after that time all the bodies that came up seemed to be women and children. It had begun to drizzle just before the boat was to start, and the mothers had taken their children inside to be out of the wet. In the meantime my sister was looking for me in the morgues and at Reid & Murdoch's. Someone had telephoned to my home that I had been seen climbing over the side of the boat and had fallen off. I was working over a man down at the warehouse when I heard someone scream, 'My God, it's Helen!' It was my sister. She fainted when she saw me."

Finally it was obvious that there was little else to be accomplished. Repa concluded her harrowing tale: "When I started out in the morning I had had on a white uniform and white shoes. By noon, what with dressing wounds and kneeling on the dock, I was covered with bloodstains and caked with mud from head to foot. I had lost my coat. A fireman threw a woman's skirt over my shoulders, and I kept the rain out with that. At four o'clock I went home. There was nothing left to do. I had been on my feet since seven-thirty that morning, and I felt that if I ever sat down I would never get up again. I came home in the street car, with the skirt wrapped around my shoulders and my brother's raincoat over that."

Pictures of victims being pulled from the wreck

A picture of a building full of victims

In the midst of the larger tragedy was a smaller one, as the *Chicago Daily Tribune* reported on a little boy who no one came to claim: "'Whose little boy is that?' Almost every one seeking relatives or friends at the Second Regiment armory morgue has asked the question as they passed the body of a dark, curly haired boy, between 8 and 9 years old. Some mothers, looking for their own babies, have shed their tears over him as they gazed at the little face. Sadly they have shaken their heads and asked the question. The body, numbered 396, has been there since 4 o'clock Saturday afternoon. The boy had been dressed all in white."

Eventually, the boy was finally identified. The paper reported, "THIS LITTLE EASTLAND VICITM IS IDENTIFIED AT LAST. Two boys yesterday identified body No 396 as Willie Novotny, their 7 year old playmate." When 13,000 people from the city showed up to bury him, Mayor Big Bill Thompson said movingly, "The hearts of all Chicagoans go out in grief to the sufferers from this calamity. The city mourns."

Chapter 6: Strong Evidence

"The federal prosecutors had very strong evidence. More than eight hundred deaths, a steamship capsized while still tied to its dock. No act of God. No iceberg. No torpedo. Two chief engineers of the Eastland confessed to investigators in Chicago that the ship owners had discussed stability problems in 1914 and 1915. ... There was a history of near-accidents on the Eastland going back a dozen years. Surely, the owners were negligent if they didn't bother to learn about them. ... In front of the coroner's jury in Chicago, Steele— the self-proclaimed angel of the Eastland's company— lied repeatedly. As to the government's steamboat-inspection service, it simply didn't connect the dots as the Eastland moved from Lake Michigan to Lake Erie and then back. The inspectors themselves set off red flags, then failed to follow them up. In the next ten days, the captain would weep on the stand, and the two sides would clash over everything, even whether the Chicago River technically existed anymore. ... Now, seven months after the disaster, was the moment for justice. There was surely criminal misconduct with such a horrific number of wrongful deaths. The guilty would surely be exposed. Long penitentiary sentences were surely coming— unless the defense could somehow outduel the prosecutors." - Michael McCarthy, *Ashes Under Water: The SS Eastland and the Shipwreck That Shook America.*

A picture of the *Eastland* being righted after the disaster

Within days of the disaster, a coroner's jury was convened to hear the evidence about what went wrong with the *Eastland* and render an opinion about what, if anything, should be done. During the hearing, Greenbaum was questioned extensively on whether or not he felt the government inspections were sufficient for ensuring that the ships plying the Great Lakes were safe for passengers. He replied, "We have to apply for a certificate in the spring. The inspection certificate is given for one year's time. They come over and examine the boat, and if they find everything O. K., they give a certificate to operate for the year, and then they make occasional inspections to see that everything is in good order. ... The Government steamboat boiler inspector has to thoroughly examine and see that all mechanical apparatus aboard the steamer conforms with the Government rules and regulations. The Government — the boiler inspector, I presume, is the one that prepares the questions which the men have to answer when they get their license. I believe the boiler inspector and the hull inspector jointly sign the license. [The inspector] should be a man well versed in everything pertaining to it. He should have graduated from the ranks, started as a coal passer, fireman, gone up through as oiler, fireman, first, second and third assistant. ... A hull inspector — his mode of advancement would be to start as a seaman, as a lookout, wheelsman, on up to mate, then to captain. ... At the present time there are three certificates each…One given to the collector of customs, one is given to the boat, and it is retained in the office of the inspectors."

Greenbaum was also questioned about other inspections his company made to their vessels. He added, "We carry insurance on the boats and the insurance representatives at different intervals come down and inspect the steamers when we have the boats in the dry dock ; they always come there to see that everything is fit and proper. We put the boats in dock — dry dock — each spring, to be sure that everything is right. They always have men down there."

Since overcrowding was considered one of the contributing factors in the Eastland *incident*, the coroner's jury questioned Greenbaum about how ships were given information regarding the number of passengers they could carry. He told them, "The Government regulation provides for a certain number of passengers between the 15th of May and the 15th of October; in addition, it provides for a number after that period; then if you alter your boat at all during the year, put on additional equipment, you make an application to the inspector. There is not only inspectors, but the Government has a boat that goes around occasionally to see whether the requirements are being complied with in order with the Government. The other day, at the time of the disaster, we threw several hundred life preservers overboard; that decreased the equipment. Before letting the Roosevelt go out the next morning I called up the steamboat inspector, and asked him, and he reduced my capacity until we got repair for the equipment that was lost. ... I think their rules were changed — I think their rules now provide they must inspect two or three times during the season of operation. ...I have seen them numerous times. They are down around the docks every Sunday; I have seen them other times. We had a large party to handle on the 28th of June; they were down; they. were on the Roosevelt about two weeks ago; they went on at Michigan City and had a fire drill over there — made them put the boats over to see that the men were acquainted with operating the life-boats."

Next, the jury inquired about the training that those in charge of the ships received. Greenbaum assured them, "The captain and the engineer are required to see that their subordinates are — that they have their proper papers. As I recall, it is punishable by fine if they do not; then there is a space on the boat where the license must be exhibited for public inspection. We have three spaces for engineers and the same number for the captain and the mates. ... We presume the Government, in issuing a license, knows they are competent. In the selection of our men we determine their past record, their general reputation."

Greenbaum also discussed the method of loading the steamer: "In unloading passengers, the ballast, would be to take the water out, so that would bring the boat up and putting the passengers, to hold the boat stable. My idea would be to have the water in her. I supposed the water was in it on the outer. My idea was that the water — my idea was that they were to hold the water over on the left side, so as to raise the gangway to make it easier of access to the passengers to come aboard. ...the tendency of the people when they go aboard is to stay on the side where their friends are coming down the dock, so that would take the water on the outside, so the reason to trim the tank so as to offset the weight on that side."

Finally, Greenbaum had to provide an answer for why the *Eastland* capsized, and while he conceded he could give no definitive answer, he did speculate on a couple of possibilities: "Why, one would have been the matter of having the ballast in her hull properly, I believe if the boat had been filled with water, she wouldn't have gone over, and other one would have been the question of having too much water on one side, and another would have been if the boat listed over, the portholes down in the hull might have been closed and the water gone in, and another one would have been the question of a great deal of weight, that is, the body of the people going over on one side, and another one would have been, but this didn't happen, because the tug hadn't started to pull her out."

As a result of this and other testimony, the grand jury issued indictments for manslaughter against the president of the steamship company and three other officers associated with the company. It also indicted Captain Pedersen and his engineer for criminal carelessness.

A picture of Captain Pedersen

Ultimately, the men were never brought to trial after a court found "barely a scintilla of proof" with which to proceed. Instead, those who lost loved ones in the disaster had to be satisfied with the comfort that could only come from time. Meanwhile, the world moved on, mostly engulfed in the war then spreading across Europe. In fact, the *Eastland* would eventually be salvaged and converted into the USS *Wilmette*, a naval gunboat, and when the papers began to carry stories of thousands killed in a single battle, the 800+ folks who died that day in Chicago all too quickly faded from memory.

A picture of the USS *Wilmette*

A marker commemorating the *Eastland*

Online Resources

Video footage of the *Eastland* disaster can be found online at
http://www.chicagotribune.com/news/daywatch/chi-eastland-disaster-film-footage-20150208-htmlstory.html

The Sinking of the Edmund Fitzgerald: The Loss of the Largest Ship on the Great Lakes by Charles River Editors

Other books about Chicago by Charles River Editors

Other books about famous shipwrecks by Charles River Editors

Bibliography

Bonansinga, Jay. *The Sinking of the Eastland: America's Forgotten Tragedy*, Citadel Press 2004.

Hilton, George. *Eastland: Legacy of the Titanic*, Stanford University Press 1997.

McCarthy, Michael. *Ashes Under Water: The SS Eastland and the Shipwreck that Shook America*, Lyons Press 2014.

Wachholz, Ted. *The Eastland Disaster*, Arcadia Publishing 2005.

Printed in Great Britain
by Amazon